Sparkle
&
Splash

Sparkle & Splash

Soda Fountain Favorites, Homemade Elixers & Carbonated Cocktails

Colleen Mullaney

Photography by Christopher Bain

STERLING EPICURE

New York

STERLING EPICURE
New York

An Imprint of Sterling Publishing
387 Park Avenue South
New York, NY 10016

ISBN 978-1-4549-1430-3

Distributed in Canada by Sterling Publishing
c/o Canadian Manda Group, 165 Dufferin Street
Toronto, Ontario, Canada M6K 3H6
Distributed in the United Kingdom by GMC Distribution Services
Castle Place, 166 High Street, Lewes, East Sussex, England BN7 1XU
Distributed in Australia by Capricorn Link (Australia) Pty. Ltd.
P.O. Box 704, Windsor, NSW 2756, Australia

For information about custom editions, special sales, and premium
and corporate purchases, please contact Sterling Special Sales at 800-
805-5489 or specialsales@sterlingpublishing.com.

Manufactured in China

2 4 6 8 10 9 7 5 3 1

www.sterlingpublishing.com

This book is dedicated to my family; you are the happy bubbles in my life.

To my three children, Grace, Katie, and Jack, who thought our kitchen made a cool recipe lab and think every day should be filled with taste-testing sodas of every color and bubbly combination. Their favorite chapter is, of course, the one with ice cream. Just for the record, they like beets now, but only with bubbles.

And to my husband Jack, who never minded the chaos and the mess, and is now a firm believer that cocktails taste infinitely better with bubbles.

Contents

Introduction

Everyone loves fizzy carbonated drinks, and now you can make your own fresh creations at home in a rainbow of natural colors and flavors. In fact, *Sparkle & Splash* has something for everyone's taste—classic colas, soda fountain favorites, healthy elixirs, fruit-filled delights, and colorful cocktails—that all go "pop!" Here are dozens and dozens of easy, fun recipes that will have you crafting your own homemade beverages with sunny citrus, berries galore, vibrant tropical fruits, and aromatic herbs. And not only are natural carbonated beverages healthy for you, they are healthy for the environment. Home carbonators come with canisters that can be used over and over again, thus greatly reducing the number of soda bottles and cans that end up in landfills.

Why are fizzy drinks now so popular? As more and more people follow the culinary path to fresher, tastier, seasonal foods that the "farm to table" chefs have modeled for us, we now are taking the same approach to what we drink. From the explosive trend of craft cocktails and mixology, to sodas and flavored sparkling waters, we want to make our own at home.

Growing, too, is the market and availability for countertop appliances that turn tap water into sparkling water, making it easier than ever to make the real thing in your own kitchen. Simply mix fresh soda syrup with bubbly water for a drink that's as sweet as you like, minus any artificial colors, flavors, or sweeteners.

With *Sparkle & Splash*, you'll see how easy and delicious homemade carbonated drinks can be.

Bubble Makers:
Soda Siphons & Home Carbonators

The creation of the soda siphon dates back to 1829 when two Frenchmen, looking for a way to keep soda from going flat, were able to put together a gadget that did just that. The siphon grew in popularity through the 1920's and 30's, but then fell off with the destruction of many of the siphon plants in Europe during World War II. These colorful glass vintage siphons are still popular today, particularly with antique collectors, vintage aficionados, and many bar keeps.

Today's siphon bottles come in a variety of materials—plastic, glass, aluminum, and stainless steel. Some have brass heads, some are made of various composites; some have guarantees for a short period of time, while others have guarantees for life. All these variables determine price, but what they all have in common is simplicity of use. You simply fill the bottle with water, store it in the refrigerator until the water is cold, and then, just before using, you insert a CO_2 charger and press the lever. *Voila!* (as the proud creators would say), you have instant carbonation.

Home carbonators and soda makers can be much more costly, depending on the brand, size, and accessories. They come with their own carbonation methods and disposable pressurized CO2 cartridges that screw into the siphon to release the gas. When you're shopping around, look for one that is price friendly, easy to clean, dishwasher safe, and fits on your countertop. If you're an adventurous kitchen type, you might choose one without warranties (those limit you to using water or pre-approved mixes), giving you the freedom to put just about anything in the bottle.

Often stores have machines available for testing. Take advantage of this and look for a taste that is consistent, keeps its effervescence, and is light, bright, and tingly.

And, of course, there is always bottled seltzer from the grocery store, which can be used for all of the recipes in this book.

Tools of the Trade

Paring knife	Peeler	Microplane zester
Potato masher	Blender/immersion blender	Cocktail shaker
Bar glass	Muddler	Long-handled spoons, slotted spoons
Measuring cups and spoons	Saucepan	Airtight containers and Mason jars for storing
Fine mesh strainer	Pitcher and drinks dispenser	Soda siphon or home carbonation machine

The Short and Sweet of Sugars

Local honey has far more flavor than mass-produced varieties. Look for it at farm stands and specialty markets. Honey is a bit richer than sugar, and its color can vary from brand to brand.

Agave nectar (or syrup) is produced from a succulent plant that is also used to make tequila. Agave is an all-natural super-sweet syrup that allows you to use a smaller quantity than sugar. And, it dissolves easily, making it ideal to work with when mixing up liquids.

Coconut palm sugar is a natural product made from the nectar of the coconut palm tree. It has a rich flavor and a layered taster similar to molasses. It is available in most grocery stores.

Granulated sugar is the most common and popular kind of sweetener. It comes from sugar cane and is what we see lining the aisles of the grocery stores. Look for organic cane sugar, which is widely available in stores.

Stevia is a natural low calorie sweetener that's available in liquid and powdered form. It is a derivative of herbs and shrubs in the sunflower family.

Turbinado sugar, a brown sugar, is considered raw in that it has been partially processed; only the surface molasses has been washed off. It has a light brown color.

Light brown sugar and dark brown sugar are more intense in flavor due to their molasses content. Both tend to clump because they contain more moisture than white sugar.

The Fresh Fixings

Fresh organic fruit is always best. The rule here is: the fresher, the better. Choose fruit that is ripe and in season for maximum flavor.

Frozen organic fruit is the next best thing. Look for and use fruit that is not packed or processed with added sugar or syrups.

Fruit juices should always be 100 percent juice with no added sugar or preservatives.

Nectars are muddled fruits that are turned into a thick pulp or juice. They are available in a wide range of fruits: passion fruit, papaya, guava, and mango. You can find them in the international aisle of the grocery store.

The Classics

Duplicating the taste of the classic sodas isn't that hard, really. It just requires the right (fresh, ripe) ingredients mixed together with seltzer. While the taste might not be a perfect match, these sodas are made with all-natural ingredients and no dyes, high fructose corn syrups, or artificial additives. With healthy living at the forefront of everyone's agenda, this just make sense.

Cola Syrup/ Cola

This recipe will have you experiencing a Throwback Thursday from your childhood. Once you get the hang of the recipe, I guarantee you'll opt to go the homemade route over the store-bought one every time.
Makes 2 cups syrup

3 cups water

Grated zest and juice of one lemon

Grated zest and juice of one lime

Grated zest and juice of 2 oranges

2 cinnamon sticks, broken in smaller pieces

1 tablespoon dried bitter orange peel

1 teaspoon dried cilantro seeds

¼ teaspoon ground nutmeg

½ teaspoon ground ginger

1 teaspoon gum Arabic (optional)

2 cups raw sugar

3 tablespoons brown sugar

2 teaspoons vanilla extract

In a medium pot, combine the water, lemon zest, lime zest, orange zest, cinnamon sticks, bitter orange peel, cilantro, nutmeg, ginger, and gum Arabic (if using). Bring to a boil over high heat, stirring until the gum Arabic is dissolved. Add in the sugar and brown sugar, stirring until the sugar has dissolved. Remove from heat and stir in the vanilla and fruit juices. Let cool.

Strain the syrup through a fine mesh sieve and pour into an airtight container. Syrup keeps in the refrigerator for up to 1 week.

To make a glass of cola: Pour ⅓ cup cola syrup into a tall glass, add seltzer, and mix gently. Add ice and serve.

Cherry Cola
(a bit like the doctor)

The Maraschino cherry liquid gives this soda a distinctly edgy flavor. For a sweeter result, add a tablespoon of cherry liquid from the jar.

⅓ cup cola syrup (page 17)

2 tablespoons Maraschino cherry liquid, or more to taste

1½ cups seltzer

Maraschino cherries for garnish

Pour the syrup into a tall glass, add the Maraschino cherry liquid, and top with seltzer. Mix gently and serve. Garnish with a cherry, if desired.

Cherry Syrup/ Cherry Soda

Delightfully refreshing, this cherry syrup makes a zippy cherry soda. It is perfect for picnics in the park, alfresco movie nights, or backyard barbeques. **Makes 1 cup syrup**

2 cups cherries, fresh or frozen

1 teaspoon bitter orange peel

1 cup water

⅓ cup raw sugar

1 teaspoon vanilla extract

Combine the cherries, bitter orange peel, water, and sugar in a medium saucepan, bring to a boil over high heat, and boil until the sugar dissolves. Reduce the heat to medium and cook for about 15 minutes, or until the cherries are very soft. Remove from heat and stir in the vanilla extract. Mash the cherries using a potato masher.

Let mixture cool, then strain through a fine-mesh sieve into a bowl. Discard the cherries. Pour the syrup into an airtight container and store in the refrigerator for up to 2 weeks.

To make a glass of cherry soda: Pour ⅓ cup cherry syrup into a tall glass, top with seltzer and ice, and stir gently. Garnish with a cherry and serve.

Ginger Syrup/ Ginger Ale

Zesty and bubbly, this makes a satisfying soda. Ginger syrup is also perfect for sweetening iced tea, hot tea, or mixed with whiskey, bourbon, or rum. **Makes 2 cups syrup**

3 cups water

½ cup ginger root, peeled and finely chopped

1 tablespoon ground ginger

1 cup coconut palm sugar

1 tablespoon freshly squeezed lime juice

Combine the water, fresh ginger, ground ginger, and sugar in a medium saucepan. Bring to a boil, stirring until the sugar is completely dissolved; then reduce heat and simmer for 20 minutes more. Remove pan from heat, add lime juice, and strain through a fine mesh sieve into a bowl. Let the ginger syrup cool; then store in airtight containers in the refrigerator for up to 2 weeks.

To make a glass of ginger ale: Pour 3 tablespoons of ginger syrup into a tall glass, add seltzer, and mix gently. Add ice cubes and serve.

Shirley Temple

As legend has it, a bartender at Chasen's, then a famous West Hollywood gathering place for the entertainment industry, mixed up this sweet concoction and served it to a little red-haired girl with ringlets and cherry cheeks. It is today still a favorite with children the world over. **Serves 1**

Ginger ale (see recipes on page 20 for ginger syrup and ginger ale)

2 tablespoons Maraschino cherry juice (from the jar)

Cherries for garnish

Fill a tall glass with ginger ale and stir in Maraschino cherry juice. Garnish with cherries and serve.

Root Beer Syrup/ Root Beer Soda

Root 'n toot all-natural root beer syrup! You'll find the extracts at health food stores and online. At first, they may seem totally foreign and not worth the effort, but I can't tell you how many times I've made this syrup at my house. **Makes 2 cups syrup**

4 cups water

1 teaspoon dried cilantro seeds

2 star anise pods

2 cloves

¼ cup sassafras extract

2 tablespoons burdock root extract

¼ cup dark molasses

2 cups raw sugar

¼ teaspoon or 2 drops wintergreen extract

Combine the water, cilantro seeds, star anise, cloves, sassafras, and burdock root extract in a medium saucepan. Bring to a boil and let simmer 20 minutes. Add the molasses and simmer 10 minutes more. Strain the mixture through a fine-mesh sieve into a bowl, discarding bits in sieve. Pour syrup back into the pan, add sugar, and simmer 5 minutes, stirring until the sugar is dissolved.

Add wintergreen extract. Remove pan from heat and let the syrup cool. Pour the root beer syrup into airtight containers and store in the refrigerator for up to 6 weeks.

To make a glass of root beer soda: Pour ⅓ cup of root beer syrup (recipe above) in a tall glass, add seltzer, and stir gently. Add ice and serve.

Lemon Lime Syrup/
Lemon Lime Soda

Hands down, my kids' favorite soda, we make batches of this syrup all year long. Try adding a bit of cherry juice for a festive holiday inspired soda. **Makes 2 cups syrup**

1 cup water

¾ cup coconut palm sugar

Grated zest and juice of 4 limes

Grated zest and juice of 3 lemons

Combine the water, sugar, and zests in a medium saucepan, bring to a boil, and stir until sugar is dissolved. Add juices and let simmer for 20 minutes, stirring occasionally. Remove from heat and let syrup cool for one hour. Strain syrup through a fine-mesh sieve into an airtight container and store in the refrigerator for up to 2 weeks.

To make a glass of lemon-lime soda:
Pour 3 tablespoons of lemon-lime syrup into a tall glass, add seltzer, and stir gently. Add ice, garnish with lemon and lime wedges, and serve.

Orange Syrup/
Orange Soda

I like using blood oranges for the deep rich orange color. Seville oranges work well for their deep floral zest. I've also used Cava oranges, which are lighter and have a bit of a grapefruit brightness. Ultimately, using what's in season will yield the best results. **Makes 1½ cups syrup**

Grated zest and juice of 2 blood oranges

Grated zest and juice of 2 navel oranges

Zest from 1 lime

⅔ cup honey or 1 cup sugar

½ teaspoon citric acid (optional)

Combine orange zests, orange juices, lime zest, and honey (or sugar) in a saucepan over medium heat. Bring to a boil, stirring until the sugar dissolves. Stir in the citric acid. Remove pan from heat and let cool to room temperature. Strain syrup through a fine-mesh sieve into a bowl. Pour the orange syrup into airtight containers and store in the refrigerator for up to 2 weeks.

To make a glass of orange soda: Pour ⅓ cup of orange syrup into a tall glass, add seltzer, and stir gently. Add ice, garnish with an orange slice, and serve.

Cream Syrup/
Cream Soda

This is one of the easiest recipes to make and one of the most refreshing. Be sure to use vanilla beans instead of vanilla extract. Supreme ingredients make all the difference! **Makes 1 cup syrup**

2 vanilla beans, split and seeded

1½ cups sugar

1¼ cups water

Juice of 1 lemon

Cut the vanilla beans in half lengthwise and use a knife to scrape the black seeds from the bean. Transfer the seeds and bean pods to a medium saucepan. Add the sugar and water and bring to a boil over high heat, stirring until all of the sugar is dissolved. Add the lemon juice. Remove the pan from heat and let the cream syrup cool for 1 hour. Discard the vanilla bean and seeds. Pour the cream syrup into an airtight container and store in the refrigerator for up to 3 weeks.

To make a glass of cream soda: Pour 3 tablespoons of cream syrup into a tall glass, add seltzer, and stir gently. Add ice and serve.

Orange Cream Soda

This tastes like a creamsicle—yum!

For a glass of orange cream soda: Pour 1 tablespoon of orange syrup (page 24) and 2 tablespoons of cream syrup (page 26) into a tall glass, add seltzer, and stir gently. Add ice and serve.

Grapefruit Syrup/ Fresca

When I was growing up, this syrup was always stocked in my grandmother's refrigerator, and it was brought out during "happy hour" for the kids. Only later did I learn that it had grapefruit in it! I just thought it tasted like heaven. **Makes 1½ cups syrup**

1 cup coconut palm sugar

¾ cup water

2 ruby red grapefruits, zest, and juice

Combine the sugar, water, and grapefruit zest in a medium saucepan, bring to a boil, stirring until the sugar is dissolved, and add the juice. Reduce the heat and simmer 10 minutes more. Remove the pan from the heat and let cool to room temperature. Strain the syrup through a fine-mesh sieve into a bowl and discard zest. Pour the syrup into airtight containers and store in the refrigerator for up to 2 weeks.

To make a glass of Fresca: Pour 2 tablespoons grapefruit syrup into a tall glass, add seltzer, and stir gently. Add ice, garnish with a grapefruit wedge, and serve.

Grape Syrup/ Grape Soda

There is nothing better than a tall glass of grape soda! I find that chefs and mixologists recently have been using Concord grapes for their intense, rich flavor and color, but realizing that they are mostly available in the fall, I went straight for the juice, as it is available year-round. **Makes 1½ cups syrup**

3 cups organic Concord grape juice

2 tablespoons freshly squeezed lemon juice

Combine the grape juice and lemon juice in a medium saucepan, bring to a boil over medium high heat, and stir until mixture is reduced and becomes thick and syrupy, about 10 minutes. Check frequently as the grape mixture goes from syrup to singed in no time! Remove from heat and let cool. Pour the grape syrup into airtight containers and store in the refrigerator for up to 1 week.

To make a glass of grape soda: Pour 3 tablespoons Concord grape syrup into a tall glass, add seltzer, and stir gently. Add ice, garnish with fresh grapes if desired, and serve.

Lime Syrup/Limeade

This is a bit on the zesty side to satisfy those with a less extensive sweet tooth. Put the limeade in the blender with extra ice for a cooling treat on a sweltering summer day. **Makes 1½ cups syrup**

1 cup sugar

¾ cup water

Grated zest and juice of 3 limes

Lime slices for garnish

Combine sugar, water, and zest in a medium saucepan, bring to a boil, stirring until the sugar is dissolved, and add the juice. Reduce the heat and simmer until mixture is slightly reduced, about 5 minutes. Remove the pan from the heat, strain the syrup through a fine-mesh sieve into a bowl, and let the syrup cool. Pour the lime syrup into airtight containers and store in the refrigerator for up to 1 week.

To make a glass of limeade: Pour 3 tablespoons of lime syrup into a tall glass, add seltzer, and mix gently. Add ice, garnish with a lime wedge, and serve.

Lemon Syrup/ Sparkling Lemonade

Try a big batch of this sunny citrus concoction on your lemonade stand. It is sure to be a hit, with almost guaranteed record sales! **Makes 1½ cups syrup**

Zest and juice of 4 lemons

1 cup sugar

¾ cup water

Combine zest, sugar, and water in a medium saucepan, and bring to a boil, stirring until the sugar is dissolved. Remove the pan from the heat and let cool to room temperature. Stir in the lemon juice and let the syrup stand for 10 minutes. Strain the syrup through a fine-mesh sieve into a bowl. Pour the syrup into an airtight container and store in the refrigerator for up to a week.

To make sparkling lemonade: Pour 3 tablespoons lemon syrup into a tall glass, top with seltzer, and mix gently. Add ice and serve.

Raspberry Syrup/ Raspberry Lemonade

The addition of raspberries lends deep, rich flavor and bold color, giving this lemonade real character.

Makes 1 cup syrup

1½ cups raspberries

¾ cup sugar

½ cup water

Combine raspberries, sugar, and water in a small saucepan and bring to a boil over high heat, stirring until the sugar dissolves and the raspberries become soft and start falling apart, about 10 minutes. Remove the pan from the heat and let the syrup cool. Pour the syrup through a fine-mesh sieve into an airtight container and store in the refrigerator for up to 1 week.

To make a glass of raspberry lemonade: Pour 1 tablespoon of raspberry syrup and 2 tablespoons of lemon syrup (page 31) into a tall glass, add seltzer, and stir gently. Add ice, garnish with raspberries, and serve.

Strawberry Syrup/ Strawberry Lemonade

This is lemonade's sweet sister, and always a favorite at children's birthday parties. The fragrant syrup is also perfect for strawberry shortcake and on ice cream sundaes. **Makes 1 cup syrup**

1 cup strawberries, hulled and sliced

¾ cup sugar

½ cup water

Combine strawberries, sugar, and water in a small saucepan and bring to a boil over high heat, stirring until the sugar dissolves and the strawberries become soft and start to break apart, about 10 minutes. Remove the pan from the heat and let the syrup cool. Pour the syrup through a fine-mesh sieve into an airtight container and store in the refrigerator for up to 1 week.

To make strawberry lemonade: Pour 1 tablespoon strawberry syrup and 2 tablespoons lemon syrup (page 31) into a tall glass, add seltzer, and stir gently. Add ice cubes, garnish with strawberry slices, and serve.

Flavorful Spa Delights

These sodas all have clean, crisp, artisanal fresh flavors. Some tend to the exotic; others are more toward the garden patch. All have some or many health benefits to boost your immune system and refresh and feed your body.

Lavender Lemon Syrup/ Lavender Lemon Soda

Although I love rose water, lavender is more sensual with its heady aroma. When lavender is combined with lemon, it first excites, and then relaxes, your taste buds.

1 cup water

½ cup raw sugar

½ cup honey

Juice of 1 lemon

4–6 stalks lavender

Seltzer

Lemon wedges for garnish

Combine water, sugar, and honey in a medium saucepan and bring to a boil, stirring until the sugar has dissolved. Add the lemon juice and simmer for 3 minutes. Remove the pan from the heat, add the lavender stalks, and let the syrup steep until cool or up to an hour. Strain the syrup through a fine-mesh sieve into an airtight container and store in the refrigerator for up to 1 week.

To make lavender lemon soda: Pour 3 tablespoons of syrup into a glass, add seltzer, and mix gently. Add ice, garnish with a lemon wedge, and serve.

Lemongrass Syrup/ Lemongrass Soda

I love the mellow flavor of lemongrass paired with sweet coconut and a zip of ginger. This soda has exotic flair and flavors. Heat up the syrup with 1 cup of flat water for a cold-fighting remedy. **Makes 2 cups syrup**

3 or 4 plump lemongrass stalks

½ cup thinly sliced peeled ginger root

Zest and juice of 2 lemons

1 cup sugar

2 cups water

1 cup coconut nectar

Cut the top third from the lemongrass stalks and discard. Chop the remaining lemongrass into 1-inch pieces. In a medium pot, combine the lemongrass, ginger, zest, sugar, and water and bring to a boil over high heat, stirring until the sugar dissolves. Add lemon juice and coconut nectar, reduce the heat, and let simmer 10 minutes until mixture reduces a bit. Remove the pan from the heat and let the mixture steep for 1 hour. Strain the mixture through a fine-mesh sieve into a bowl. Pour the lemongrass syrup into airtight containers and store in the refrigerator up to 1 week.

To make lemongrass soda: Pour 3 tablespoons lemongrass syrup into a tall glass, add seltzer, and mix gently. Add ice, garnish with a lemon slice, and serve.

Note: When buying lemongrass, look for firm stalks. The lower stalk should be pale yellow (almost white) in color, while the upper stalks are green. Usually fresh lemongrass is sold in groupings of 3 or 4 stalks. Look for fresh lemongrass at your local grocery store or Asian market. If you can't find it with the fresh produce, check the freezer section; lemongrass stalks are also sold in frozen packets.

Acai Berry Syrup/ Acai Berry Soda

Acai berries are small, dark purple berries from the Amazon rainforest in Brazil. They boost energy and have antioxidants, amino acids, and omega fatty acids that are shown to help slow the aging process. All that in a little purple berry! The frozen or freeze-dried acai berries have the most antioxidant potency. You can find the frozen berries in specialty grocery stores and health food stores. **Makes 1 cup syrup**

1 cup acai berries

¾ cup water

¼ cup coconut palm sugar

Combine the berries, water, and sugar in a medium saucepan and bring to a boil over high heat, stirring until sugar dissolves. Reduce the heat and simmer the mixture for about 10 minutes more, mashing the berries as it simmers to create a pulp-like syrup. Remove the pan from the heat and let the syrup cool completely. Strain the syrup through a fine-mesh sieve into an airtight container and store in the refrigerator for up to 2 weeks.

To make acai berry soda: Pour 3 tablespoons of acai berry syrup into a tall glass, add seltzer, and mix gently. Add ice and serve.

Vitamin Mix/
Vitamin Water

Boost your vitamin intake instantly with this refreshing libation. You really can make this using any fresh juice or nectar you'd like. I had passion fruit nectar on hand, so I used that and it quickly became one of my favorites. **Makes 1 batch**

1 tablespoon liquid multi-vitamin supplement

Juice of 1 orange or ½ cup juice or nectar

2 teaspoons honey

Mix all ingredients in a glass until blended.

To make one glass of vitamin water: Pour vitamin mix into a glass, add seltzer, and mix gently. Add ice, garnish with an orange peel, and serve.

Mint Syrup/Mint Soda

Easy to make, mint syrup is perfect when combined with lemonades, limeades, and a variety of cocktails. I make this all the time for mojitos and cucumber mint cocktails.

Mint comes in so many different varieties: peppermint, apple-mint, orange mint, lemon mint, pineapple mint, chocolate mint, and spearmint. Mint is good for you! It has vitamins A and C and has antioxidant properties, it aids in digestion, and its scent can have a calming effect. So be calm, and mint on! **Makes 1 cup syrup**

1 cup sugar

1 cup water

1 bunch mint, plus sprigs for garnish

Combine the sugar and water in a medium saucepan and bring to a boil over high heat, stirring until the sugar dissolves. Add the mint leaves and remove the pan from the heat. Let the mixture steep for 1 hour. Strain through a fine-mesh sieve into a bowl, discarding the mint leaves. Pour the syrup into an airtight container and store in the refrigerator for up to 2 weeks.

To make a glass of mint soda: Pour 3 tablespoons of mint syrup into a tall glass, add seltzer, and stir gently. Add ice, garnish with mint sprig, and serve.

Cucumber Mint Soda

The cucumber brings a refreshing cool element to the mint, and the bubbles bring out the flavors. It's like a spa treatment in a glass! **Makes 1 serving**

3 cucumber slices

3 tablespoons mint syrup (page 40)

1 teaspoon freshly squeezed lime juice

Seltzer

Place 3 slices of cucumber, mint syrup, and lime juice into a thick glass and muddle the ingredients together. Add seltzer and stir gently to mix. Add ice, garnish with mint sprig, and serve.

Ginseng Syrup/ Ginseng Soda

Ginseng is a natural herb linked to helping with memory, alertness, and energy. It comes in a few forms: the root, powder, root capsules, and tea. Most health food stores carry a few of these varieties, and it is available online. The tea generally is much milder than the powder. Here, I've added honey for a spot of needed sweetness. **Makes ¾ cup syrup**

1½ teaspoons ginseng powder

¾ cup coconut palm sugar

1 cup water

Zest and juice of 1 lemon

3 tablespoons honey

Combine ginseng powder, sugar, water lemon zest, and honey in a medium saucepan and bring to a boil over high heat, stirring until the sugar dissolves. Remove the pan from the heat, stir in lemon juice, and let the syrup steep for 30 minutes. Strain the syrup through a fine-mesh sieve into an airtight container and store in the refrigerator for up to 2 weeks.

To make a glass of ginseng soda:
Pour 3 tablespoons of ginseng syrup into a glass, add seltzer, and mix gently. Add ice, garnish with a lemon wedge, and serve.

Cinnamon Vanilla Syrup/**Cinnamon Vanilla Soda**

Warm and spicy, this soda has strong fragrant notes, but finishes with a smooth vanilla sweet touch.
Makes 1¼ cups syrup

2 tablespoons ground cinnamon	Combine the ground cinnamon, cinnamon sticks, water, and sugars in a medium saucepan and bring to a boil over high heat, stirring until the sugars dissolve. Add vanilla extract and let the mixture simmer 5 minutes more. Remove the pan from the heat and let the syrup cool completely. Strain the syrup through a fine-mesh sieve into an airtight container and store in the refrigerator for up to 2 weeks.
2 cinnamon sticks	
2 cups water	
1 cup raw sugar	
½ cup light brown sugar	
3 tablespoons vanilla extract	**To make a glass of cinnamon vanilla soda:** Pour ⅓ cup of syrup into a glass, add seltzer, and mix gently. Add ice and serve.

Jalapeno Syrup/
Jalapeno Soda

How about a little heat in your soda? Jalapenos are trendy and the hotter the better. They have a good amount of vitamin A. Here's to a spicy soda with a balance of sweetness and heat. **Makes 1 cup syrup**

2 jalapeno peppers, thinly sliced with seeds

Juice of 3 limes

¾ cup sugar

¾ cup water

Lime for garnish

Combine jalapeno pepper, lime juice, sugar, and water in a medium pan and bring to a boil over medium high heat, stirring until the sugar dissolves. Remove the pan from the heat and let the syrup cool completely. Strain the syrup through a fine-mesh sieve into an airtight container and store in the refrigerator for up to 1 week.

To make jalapeno soda: Pour 3 tablespoons of jalapeno syrup into a glass, add seltzer, and mix gently. Add ice, garnish with a lime wedge, and serve. Spicy pepper goes perfectly with the sweetness of grapefruit and watermelon. Here's a few to try:

Jalapeno Grapefruit Soda

Add ½ cup grapefruit juice to the syrup; then add the seltzer and mix gently. Add ice and serve.

Jalapeno Watermelon Soda

Purée 1 cup watermelon chunks in a blender or food processor. Pour the watermelon juice into a glass, add jalapeno syrup and seltzer, and mix gently. Add ice and serve.

Prune Syrup/ Prune Rosemary Soda

Prunes protect against free radical damage and help with digestion and the protection of skin cells. Spicy notes from rosemary blend well with the full rich taste of the prune juice. **Makes 2 cups syrup**

4 cups prune juice

¼ cup agave nectar

3 rosemary sprigs

½ cup water

Combine all ingredients in a medium saucepan and bring to a boil over medium heat, stirring until the sugar dissolves. Continue to simmer until the mixture reduces by one third.

Remove the pan from the heat and let the syrup cool completely. Strain the prune syrup through a fine-mesh sieve into a bowl, discarding solids. Pour the syrup into airtight containers and store in the refrigerator for up to 2 weeks.

To make a glass of prune rosemary soda: Pour 4 tablespoons of syrup into a glass, add seltzer, and mix gently. Add ice, garnish with a rosemary sprig, and serve.

Pomegranate Syrup/
Pomegranate Soda

Pomegranates are sky high in antioxidants. You can make juice from pomegranate seeds, but that is labor intensive. Here, I simply use the store-bought juice to make the syrup. So drink up! **Makes 2 cups syrup**

4 cups pomegranate juice	Combine the pomegranate juice, agave nectar, and water in a medium saucepan and bring to a boil, stirring occasionally. Reduce the heat, add the lime juice, and simmer until the liquid has reduced by half and begins to thicken. Remove the pan from the heat and let the syrup cool completely. Pour the syrup into airtight containers and store in the refrigerator for up to 6 months.
¼ cup agave nectar	
½ cup water	
Juice of 1 lime	

To make a glass of pomegranate soda: Pour 3 tablespoons of pomegranate syrup into a glass, add seltzer, and mix gently. Add ice and serve.

Coconut Syrup/ Coconut Soda

Simple but so delicious, coconut soda has a shot of tropical sweetness in every sip. For a lighter version, substitute coconut milk for the nectar. **Makes 1 cup syrup**

1 cup raw sugar

½ cup water

2 cups coconut nectar

Combine sugar, water, and coconut nectar in a medium saucepan and bring to a boil over medium heat, stirring until the sugar dissolves. Remove from heat and let the syrup cool completely.

To make a glass of coconut soda:
Pour ⅓ cup coconut syrup into a glass, add seltzer, and mix gently. Add ice and serve.

Peach Lychee Syrup/
Peach Lychee Soda

A sweet herbal syrup, peach lychee syrup ideally should be made with fresh summer peaches, but during the cooler months, frozen peaches are the next best thing. This syrup is perfect for adding to sparkling water, lemonade, or iced tea. **Makes 2 cups syrup**

4 cups fresh or frozen peaches, cut into chunks

½ cup sugar

1 can lychee fruit

Zest and juice of 1 lime

Combine peaches, sugar, lychee fruit, and zest into a medium saucepan and bring to a boil over medium heat, stirring until the sugar dissolves. Reduce the heat to medium, add lime juice, and continue to simmer the mixture, mashing or muddling the peaches and lychee into a pulp. Remove the pan from the heat and let the syrup cool. Strain the syrup through a fine-mesh sieve into a bowl. Pour the syrup into airtight bottles or glass jars and store in the refrigerator for up to 1 week.

To make a glass of peach lychee soda: Pour ⅓ cup of syrup into a glass, add seltzer, and stir gently. Add ice and serve.

Ginger Beet Syrup/ Ginger Beet Soda

For centuries, chefs have used beets for their natural sweet goodness. Striking beet colors make for an exciting, unique soda with an arresting flavor. **Makes 2 cups syrup**

2 cups chopped beets

¼ cup ginger root, peeled and sliced

4 cups organic apple juice

Combine beets, ginger, and apple juice in a medium saucepan and bring to a boil over high heat. Reduce the heat and simmer the mixture for 20 minutes, or until liquid is reduced by half. As the beets become soft, mash them with a potato masher. Remove the pan from the heat and let the syrup cool completely. Strain the syrup through a fine-mesh sieve into a bowl, discarding solids. Pour the syrup into airtight containers and store it in the refrigerator for up to 2 weeks.

To make a glass of ginger beet soda: Pour 3 tablespoons of ginger beet syrup into a glass, add seltzer, and mix gently. Add ice and serve.

Cayenne Agave Syrup/
Cayenne Agave Soda

Now you can make your own cleansing soda; it's easy enough to make as part of your regular diet.

1 teaspoon cayenne powder

Juice of 1 lemon

2 teaspoons agave nectar

½ cup water

Combine the powder, juice, agave nectar, and water in a small saucepan and simmer, stirring until everything is blended. Remove the pan from the heat and let the syrup cool completely.

To make a glass of cayenne soda:
Pour cayenne syrup into a glass, add seltzer, and mix gently. Add ice and serve.

Kiwi Syrup/ Kiwi Soda

Beautiful light green color explodes from this refreshing sparkler. It is perfect for an everyday libation as well as a special celebration. **Makes ¾ cup syrup.**

4 ripe kiwis, peeled and chopped

Juice of 1 lime

¼ cup agave nectar

In a blender or food processor combine the kiwis, lime juice, and agave nectar and purée until smooth. Pour into an airtight container and store in the refrigerator for up to 3 days.

To make a glass of kiwi soda: Pour ¾ cup of kiwi mixture into a glass and add seltzer. Mix gently and serve.

Grapefruit Orange Syrup/Grapefruit Orange Soda

Filled with a floral like fragrance and a honey aroma, this libation is a crowd pleaser. The blended citrus is divine. **Makes 1½ cups syrup**

Zest and juice of 2 pink grapefruits

Zest and juice of 1 blood orange

2 cups sugar

½ cup water

Juice of 1 lemon

Combine zests, sugar, and water in a medium saucepan and bring to a boil over medium heat, stirring until the sugar dissolves. Add the juices, reduce the heat, and simmer a few minutes more. Remove the pan from the heat and let the syrup steep for 1 hour. Strain the syrup through a fine-mesh sieve into a bowl. Pour the syrup into an airtight container and store in the refrigerator for up to 2 weeks.

To make a glass of grapefruit orange soda: Pour 3 tablespoons of grapefruit orange syrup into a glass, add seltzer, and mix gently. Add ice cubes, garnish with a grapefruit wedge, and serve.

Fruit Market

Fresh fruit lends itself to sweet and juicy results in the kitchen. With sun-ripened seasonally fresh fruit, you'll have a bumper crop of summer in every sip using the recipes in this chapter and the next.

Ginger Pear Syrup/ Ginger Pear Soda

Pears lend themselves to this crisp, clean soda. They have a delicate floral, extremely nuanced flavor with a gentle aroma and a light honey color.

Makes 1⅓ cups syrup

3 ripe pears such as Bosc, Anjou, or Bartlett, cut into slices

½ cup maple syrup

¼ cup ginger, peeled and sliced

Zest and juice of 1 lemon

Combine pears, syrup, ginger, and lemon zest in a medium saucepan and bring to a boil. Reduce the heat to a simmer and simmer the mixture for 10 minutes, or until the pears are soft. Add the lemon juice and remove from heat. Mash the pears with a potato masher until pulpy. Strain mixture through a fine-mesh sieve in to an airtight container and store in the refrigerator for up to 1 week.

To make a glass of ginger pear soda: Pour ¼ cup of syrup into a glass, add seltzer, and mix gently. Add ice and serve.

Strawberry Mint Syrup/Strawberry Mint Soda

This is like an instant party in your mouth, refreshing and light. The sweetness from the strawberries is instantly interrupted by the heat of the mint. **Makes 1½ cups syrup**

3 cups strawberries, hulled and halved

1 tablespoon freshly squeezed lemon juice

¾ cup water

¾ cup coconut palm sugar

8 mint leaves

Combine the strawberries, lemon juice, water, and sugar in a medium saucepan and bring to a boil over high heat, stirring until the sugar dissolves. Reduce the heat, add the mint leaves, and simmer for 10 minutes, or until the strawberries are soft. Remove the pan from the heat and mash the strawberries with a potato masher. Strain through a fine-mesh sieve into an airtight container and store in the refrigerator for up to 1 week.

To make a glass of strawberry mint soda: Put 3 tablespoons syrup in a glass, add seltzer, and mix gently. Add ice cubes, garnish with a strawberry or mint leaf, and serve.

Note: Strawberry syrup is perfect for an ice cream soda, strawberry mojitos, and champagne punch.

Mixed Berry Syrup/ Mixed Berry Soda

An explosion of freshness and deep rich flavors, bright and rich, this syrup is perfect for a soda. Try this lush syrup over ice cream or over a stack of pancakes.

3 cups mixed strawberries (that have been cut and hulled)

Blackberries, blueberries, and raspberries (fresh or frozen)

¼ cup orange juice

¾ cup coconut palm sugar

½ cup water

Combine the fruit, orange juice, sugar, and water and bring to a boil over high heat, stirring until the sugar dissolves. Reduce the heat and simmer for 10 minutes until the fruit is soft. Remove the pan from the heat and mash the fruit with a potato masher. Strain the syrup through a fine-mesh sieve into an airtight container and store in the refrigerator for up to 1 week.

To make a glass of mixed berry soda: Pour ¼ cup syrup into a glass, add seltzer, and mix gently. Add ice, garnish with fruit or mint sprig, and serve.

Raspberry Vanilla Syrup/**Raspberry Vanilla Soda**

Raspberries are pretty little eye-catching super food that regulate digestion and blood sugar and increase metabolism. They also contain anti-inflammatory properties.

This is a great soda before or after your workout. **Makes 1½ cups syrup**

2 cups raspberries	Combine the raspberries, sugar, and water in a medium saucepan and bring to a boil over high heat, stirring until the sugar dissolves. Remove the pan from heat and add the vanilla extract. Mash the raspberries into a pulp with a potato masher and let the mixture cool completely. Stain through a fine-mesh sieve into a bowl. Pour the syrup into an airtight container and store in the refrigerator for up to 2 weeks.
½ cup coconut palm sugar	
¾ cup water	
2 tablespoons vanilla extract	

To make a glass of raspberry soda: Pour ¼ cup of raspberry vanilla syrup into a glass, add seltzer, and mix gently. Add ice and serve.

Pomegranate Blueberry Syrup/ Pomegranate Blueberry Soda

This soda has a delicate sweet flavor, subtle scent of citrus, and an intense hue. It also boasts a great supply of vitamin C, so it's a great way to start the day. **Makes 1½ cups syrup**

2 cups fresh pomegranate juice

1 cup blueberries, fresh or frozen

1 cup cranberries, fresh or frozen

¼ cup raw cane sugar

½ cup apple juice

3 teaspoons freshly squeezed lime juice

Combine the pomegranate juice, blueberries, cranberries, and sugar in a medium saucepan and bring to a boil over high heat, stirring until the sugar is dissolved. Remove the pan from the heat and mash the fruit with a potato masher. Add the apple juice and lime juice and simmer over medium heat for 5 minutes. Remove the pan from the heat and let the mixture cool. Strain through a fine-mesh sieve into a bowl, discarding solids. Pour syrup into an airtight container and store in the refrigerator for up to 2 weeks.

To make a glass of pomegranate blueberry soda: Pour ¼ cup pomegranate blueberry syrup into a glass, add seltzer, and mix gently. Add ice and serve.

Blackberry Rosemary Syrup/Blackberry Rosemary Soda

Ripe jammy berries marry with herbal notes. This is a no-fuss soda, perfect for lazy afternoons on the porch or an impromptu gathering with friends. **Makes 1½ cups**

2 cups blackberries	Combine blackberries, sugar, and water in a medium saucepan, muddle the berries, and bring the mixture to a boil over medium heat, stirring until sugar dissolves. Remove the pan from the heat and add vinegar and rosemary. Return the pan to the heat and bring the mixture to a boil. Remove the pan from the heat and let the mixture cool. Pour the mixture through a fine-mesh sieve into an airtight container and store in the refrigerator for up to 2 weeks.
1 cup coconut palm sugar	
2 cups water	
½ cup balsamic vinegar	
2 sprigs rosemary	

To make a glass of blackberry rose soda: Fill a glass halfway with ice. Pour ¼ cup of blackberry syrup over the ice and add seltzer. Stir gently and serve.

Peach Basil Syrup/ Peach Basil Soda

The sweetness of the peaches is balanced divinely with the basil. It's spicy like mint, with a peppery finish. This syrup is gorgeous over a big scoop of ice cream. Or, pour a dash in the bottom of a glass, top with champagne, and enjoy. **Makes 1½ cups syrup**

3 cups peaches, sliced

½ cup raw cane sugar

½ cup water

6 basil leaves

2 teaspoons lemon juice

Combine peaches, sugar, and water in a medium saucepan and simmer over medium heat until peaches are soft and sugar is dissolved, about 10 minutes. Add basil leaves and lemon juice and mash fruit to a pulp with a potato masher. Remove the pan from the heat and let the mixture steep. Pour mixture through a fine-mesh sieve into an airtight container and store in the refrigerator for up to 2 weeks.

To make a glass of peach basil soda: Put 3 tablespoons peach basil syrup in a glass, add seltzer, and mix gently. Add ice, garnish with a peach slice, and serve.

Cherry Apple Ginger Syrup/Cherry Apple Ginger Soda

Pitting cherries is a laborious project, so I cook them whole and then mash them when they're soft. Adding apple and ginger gives this soda an upfront, bright taste, a favorite with my kids!

Note: Frozen cherries work here as well. **Makes 2 cups syrup**

2 cups cherries

½ cup coconut palm sugar or raw cane sugar

¾ cup water

¾ cup apple juice

⅛ cup peeled and sliced fresh ginger

Combine the cherries, sugar, water, apple juice, and ginger in a medium saucepan and bring to a boil, stirring until the sugar is dissolved. Remove the pan from the heat and mash the cherries with a potato masher. Strain the syrup through a fine-mesh sieve into a bowl, discarding the pits. Pour the syrup into an airtight container and store in the refrigerator for up to 2 weeks.

To make a glass of cherry apple soda: Put 3 tablespoons of syrup into a glass, add seltzer, and mix gently. Add ice and serve.

Plum Prune Syrup/ Plum Bliss

Seductive with their shape and rich colors—purple, blue, green, yellow—plums are tart and fragrant, perfect for natural sodas and cocktails.
Makes 1½ cups syrup

2 cups (about 6) plums, sliced	Combine the plums, prune juice, water, sugar, and agave nectar in a medium saucepan and bring to a boil over high heat, stirring until the sugar dissolves and plums are soft and pulpy. Remove the pan from the heat and add the vanilla extract and anise extract. Mash the plums with a potato masher. Strain the mixture through a fine-mesh sieve into an airtight container and store in the refrigerator for up to 1 week.
1 cup prune juice	
¾ cup water	
½ cup sugar	
¼ cup agave nectar	
1 teaspoon vanilla extract	**To make a glass of plum bliss:** Put ⅓ cup plum syrup into a glass, add seltzer, and mix gently. Add ice and serve.
1 teaspoon anise extract	

Note: Anise extract is the pure extraction of the licorice-scented oil of star anise.

Cinnamon Pear Syrup/ Spicy Pear Soda

Full of buttery, well rounded flavors, this syrup is divine when mixed in with oatmeal or drizzled over apple pie à la mode. For an adult adaptation, substitute pinot noir for the water and apple juice.

Makes 1½ cups syrup

3 ripe pears, such as Bosc, Anjou, or Bartlett, sliced

½ cup coconut palm sugar

¾ cup water

½ cup apple juice

2 cinnamon sticks

2 teaspoons ground cinnamon

1 teaspoon lemon juice

Combine pears, sugar, water, apple juice, cinnamon sticks, and cinnamon in a medium saucepan and bring to a boil over high heat, stirring until the sugar dissolves and the pears are soft. Add the lemon juice. Then remove the pan from the heat and mash the mixture with a potato masher into a pulp. Strain the mixture through a fine-mesh sieve into a bowl, discarding solids. Pour the syrup into an airtight container and store in the refrigerator for up to 1 week.

To make spicy pear soda: Pour ¼ cup of cinnamon pear syrup in a glass, add seltzer, and mix gently. Add ice, garnish with a slice of pear, and serve.

Apricot Thyme Syrup/
Apricot Soda

Sweet apricots have subtle flavor, so, in order to make this soda pop, I used nectar. Its concentrated flavor and crunchy brightness are wonderful. **Makes 2 cups syrup**

4 cups apricot nectar

4 sprigs thyme

Bring nectar to a boil in a medium saucepan over high heat; then add thyme. Remove the pan from the heat and let steep for up to 1 hour. Remove thyme sprigs. Pour syrup into an airtight container and store in the refrigerator for up to 1 week.

To make a glass of apricot soda:
Pour ⅓ cup apricot nectar into a glass, add seltzer, and mix gently. Add ice, garnish with a thyme sprig, and serve.

Tropical Twist

A wide variety of available nectars and tropical fruits make the mixology an endless, tasty pursuit of combinations. Nectars play a starring role here. They are available in an array of tropical flavors and can be found in most grocery stores or specialty food stores.

Pineapple Mint Syrup/ Pineapple Mint Soda

Popular in Africa, India, and tropical islands like the Bahamas, pineapple soda has been around for ages. It's naturally refreshing and a welcome coolant for the body on hot sultry days. The addition of mint adds a bit of spice to create a sweet and spicy dance party with your taste buds. **Makes 2 cups syrup**

3 cups pineapple chunks

1½ cups coconut palm sugar

1 bunch fresh mint

Juice of 1 lemon

Combine the pineapple chunks and sugar in a bowl and let stand, covered, for at least 6 hours or overnight. (This allows the fruit to release its juices and the sugar to dissolve.)

Pour the macerated pineapple mixture into a saucepan and bring to a boil. Remove the pan from the heat, add mint leaves, and let steep for 30 minutes. Pour the mixture through a fine-mesh sieve into a bowl, discarding solids. Pour syrup into airtight containers or Mason jars and store in the refrigerator for up to 2 weeks.

To make a glass of pineapple mint soda: Pour 2 oz. pineapple mint syrup into a glass, add seltzer, and mix gently. Add ice, garnish with pineapple chunks and mint sprig, and serve.

Papaya Citrus Syrup/
Papaya Citrus Soda

A subtly sweet tropical fruit, papaya originated in the south of Mexico but made its way to other tropical climes, such as Hawaii. Often found in syrup form, it is used for cooking in many dishes. **Makes 2 cups syrup**

1½ cups papaya nectar

½ cup pineapple juice

3 teaspoons freshly squeezed lime juice

2 teaspoons honey

Combine all the ingredients in a Mason jar or airtight container and store in the refrigerator for up to 4 days.

To make a glass of papaya citrus soda: Pour ⅔ cup of the papaya citrus syrup into a glass, add seltzer, and mix gently. Add ice and serve.

Mango Coconut Syrup/Mango Colada

Super refreshing and light, this soda will have you dreaming of palm trees and gently rolling turquoise waters. Try mixing all ingredients in a blender filled with ice for a frozen colada. **Makes 2 cups syrup**

1 cup mango nectar

½ cup cream of coconut

¼ cup pineapple juice

2 teaspoons freshly squeezed lime juice

¼ cup agave nectar

Combine all the ingredients in a Mason jar or an airtight container and shake well. Store in the refrigerator for up to 5 days.

To make a glass of mango colada: Pour ⅓ cup mixture into a glass, add seltzer, and mix gently. Add ice and serve.

Guava Syrup/ Guava Soda

Transport yourself to the tropics with this guava soda. The base is ideal with a bit of rum. **Makes 3½ cups**

2 cups guava nectar

1 cup crème de banana

½ cup orange juice

2 teaspoons freshly squeezed lemon juice

3 teaspoons agave nectar

Combine all the ingredients in a Mason jar or airtight container and shake well. Store in the refrigerator for up to 5 days.

To make a glass of guava soda: Pour ⅓ cup mixture in a glass, add seltzer, and mix gently. Add ice and serve.

Dragon Fruit Syrup/ Dragon Fruit Soda

Dragon fruit is a type of cactus fruit that can be found in your grocery store's exotic fruit section. Covered with magenta skin and dotted with acid-green scales, it pops vibrantly from the produce display. The mild red or white flesh is flecked with tiny black seeds. Dragon fruit is low in calories and has natural vitamins, minerals, and fiber. **Makes 1½ cups syrup**

2 dragon fruits, peeled and cut into chunks

1 cup black currant juice

¼ cup agave nectar

Juice of 2 limes

Combine all the ingredients in a blender or food processor and blend until smooth. Pour mixture through a fine-mesh sieve into an airtight container, discarding solids, and store in the refrigerator for up to 1 week.

To make a glass of dragon fruit soda: Pour ⅓ cup of dragon fruit syrup into a glass, add seltzer, and mix gently. Add ice and serve.

Kiwi Strawberry Syrup/ Kiwi Strawberry Soda

Luscious sweet strawberries and vibrant crunchy kiwis make for a winning combination. Add bubbles, and you have a top-notch soda. **Makes ¾ cup syrup**

3 kiwis, peeled and sliced

6–8 strawberries, hulled and sliced

Juice of 1 lime

2 tablespoons agave nectar

1 teaspoon vanilla extract

Combine all the ingredients in a blender or food processor and purée until smooth. Pour through a fine-mesh sieve into an airtight container and store in the refrigerator for up to 2 days.

To make a glass of kiwi strawberry soda: Pour ¼ cup kiwi strawberry syrup in a glass, add seltzer, and mix gently. Add ice, garnish with a strawberry, and serve.

Passion Fruit Syrup/
Passion Fruit Soda

Get your taste buds bubbling with this enticing and intensely scented tropical soda. **Makes 3½ cups syrup**

2 cups passion fruit nectar

1 cup crème de coconut

½ cup orange juice

Juice of 1 lime

Combine all the ingredients in a Mason jar or bowl and shake or mix well; then store in the refrigerator for up to 2 days.

To make a passion fruit soda: Pour ⅓ cup syrup into a glass, add seltzer, and mix gently. Add ice, garnish with a lime wedge, and serve.

Sparkling Agua Frescas

Spanish for "fresh waters," agua frescas are a combination of fruits, flowers, or seeds blended with sugar and water. They are popular in Mexico, Central America, the Caribbean, and the United States. While they are sold primarily by street vendors, they now are seen on menus and in the popular juice bars. The following fruits lend themselves to an agua fresca rather than a cooked, strained syrup.

Honeydew Melon Syrup/Sparkling Honeydew Agua Fresca

Makes ¾ cup syrup

1 fresh honeydew melon, cut into chunks

½ cup tangerine juice or blood orange juice

3 tablespoons agave nectar

2 tablespoons lime juice

Combine all the ingredients in a blender or food processor and blend until smooth. Pour mixture through a fine mesh sieve into an airtight container and store in the refrigerator for up to 4 days.

To make a glass of sparkling honeydew agua fresca: Pour ½ cup cantaloupe syrup into a glass, add seltzer, and mix gently. Add ice and serve.

Cantaloupe Syrup/ Sparkling Cantaloupe Agua Fresca

Makes ¾ cup syrup

1 fresh cantaloupe, cut into chunks

½ cup tangerine juice or blood orange juice

3 tablespoons agave nectar

Combine all ingredients in a blender or food processor and blend until smooth. Pour mixture through a fine-mesh sieve into an airtight container and store in refrigerator for up to 4 days.

To make a glass of sparkling cantaloupe agua fresca: Pour ½ cup cantaloupe syrup into a glass, add seltzer, and mix gently. Add ice and serve.

Watermelon Syrup/ Sparkling Watermelon Agua Fresca

Makes ½ cup watermelon syrup

4 cups watermelon cut into chunks

3 tablespoons agave nectar

Juice of 1 lime

Combine all the ingredients in a blender or food processor and blend until smooth. Pour mixture through a fine-mesh sieve into an airtight container and store in the refrigerator for up to 4 days.

To make a glass of sparkling watermelon agua fresca: Pour ½ cup watermelon mixture into a glass, add seltzer, and mix gently. Add ice and serve.

Egg Cream Sodas, Floats, and Dessert-Inspired Beverages

Because everyone needs a treat now and then, here are a few indulgences. With rich flavors and layers of deliciousness, there is something for everyone's sweet tooth.

Espresso Soda Float

A decadent dessert, this is my favorite for dinner parties and informal gatherings, and, of course, for my casual night binges while watching a favorite TV series! **Serves 1**

1 large shot of espresso

1 teaspoon agave nectar/syrup

1 large scoop vanilla ice cream

Seltzer

Add the espresso and agave syrup to a tall soda fountain glass and stir together. Add the ice cream, top with seltzer, and stir lightly. Serve immediately.

Traditional Egg Cream

Actually an eggless, creamless libation, the egg cream is a classic old-time New York concoction that was originally invented by accident in a Brooklyn, New York candy shop. The original soda was simply a mixture of chocolate syrup, milk, and seltzer, but, as you will see, the idea has morphed into lots of different flavorings. Traditionalists serve a pretzel with this soda. **Serves 1**

2 oz. chocolate syrup (recipe follows)

3 oz. milk

8 oz. seltzer

Pour the chocolate syrup into a tall glass, add the milk, and stir to combine. Top off with the seltzer to create a frothy head, and serve.

Chocolate syrup

Makes about 1½ cups

¾ cup coconut palm sugar

¾ cup unsweetened cocoa powder

½ cup water

1 cup milk

1 teaspoon vanilla extract

Combine the sugar, cocoa powder, and water in a medium saucepan and bring to a boil, whisking constantly. Remove the pan from the heat and stir in the milk and vanilla extract. Pour the syrup into an airtight container and chill before using. The syrup may be stored in the refrigerator for up to 3 days.

Strawberry Egg Cream Soda

This egg cream is a fruity version with creamy notes and a sweet effervescent finish. **Serves 1**

1 batch strawberry syrup (page 33)

3 oz. milk

8 oz. seltzer

Pour the strawberry syrup into a tall glass, add the milk, and stir to combine. Top off with the seltzer, to create a frothy head, and serve.

Banana Egg Cream

A twist on the traditional, you may want to sprinkle cinnamon sugar on top for an extra layer of flavor.
Serves 1

⅓ cup honey

2 overripe bananas, peeled and cut into chunks

1½ teaspoons vanilla extract

3 oz. milk

Seltzer

Combine the honey, bananas, and vanilla extract in a food processor or blender and blend until smooth. Pour ¾ cup of the banana purée into a tall glass, add the milk, and top off with seltzer to create a frothy head. Stir vigorously and serve.

Caramel Syrup/ Caramel Soda

It is tricky trying to get a homemade caramel sauce that melts in your mouth. But here is my best version so far; it is divine in a soda, over ice cream, or drizzled on a rum cake. **Makes 1 cup caramel syrup**

½ cup coconut palm sugar

½ light brown sugar

½ cup water

1 cup heavy cream

1½ teaspoons vanilla extract

Combine sugars and water in a medium saucepan and bring to a boil over medium high heat, stirring until the sugars dissolve. Carefully and slowly add the heavy cream and vanilla extract (the mixture will bubble up and steam), stirring constantly. Then reduce heat and simmer for 10 minutes or until the mixture starts to thicken and resemble caramel. Remove the pan from the heat and let the syrup cool slightly. Pour the syrup into an airtight container and store in the refrigerator. Warm the caramel syrup before using.

To make a glass of caramel soda:
Scoop one scoop of vanilla ice cream into a tall glass and drizzle with ½ cup caramel syrup. Top with seltzer and stir gently. Serve with a sundae spoon.

Coffee Soda Float

Roasty coffee and creamy chocolate are meant for each other. This rich indulgence makes the perfect after-dinner treat or quick pick-me-up! **Serves 1**

2 small scoops coffee ice cream (my favorite is Häagen Dazs®)

3 tablespoons chocolate syrup (page 83)

½ cup strong black coffee, at room temperature

6 oz. seltzer

Scoop coffee ice cream into a tall glass and drizzle with chocolate syrup. Add coffee and top with seltzer. Stir gently and serve with a straw and sundae spoon.

Chocolate Coconut Soda Float

This reminds me of a Mounds® bar plus ice cream. What could be better? **Serves 1**

3 tablespoons chocolate syrup (page 83)

¼ cup cream of coconut

2 scoops vanilla ice cream

Seltzer

Pour the chocolate syrup and cream of coconut into a tall glass and mix well. Scoop the ice cream over the mixture, top with seltzer, and stir gently. Serve with a straw or sundae spoon.

Dulce de Leche/Dulce de Leche Soda Float

Dulce de leche—a combination of milk and sugars that are slowly cooked until the sugars caramelize, producing a thick, creamy, intensely flavored spread—is well worth the time it takes to make. There are a few different ways to make it, but this is one of the easiest and the most foolproof. Cook it for 3 hours for a thinner syrupy consistency, 4 for a thicker sauce. The longer you cook it, the thicker it becomes.

Start with a can of sweetened condensed milk. Remove the wrapping on the outside of the can. Then pierce 3 holes on the top of the can.

Place the can in a saucepan and fill the pan with water three-quarters of the way up the side of the can. Bring the water to a simmer and cook for 3 hours. To remove from heat, use tongs and place can on cooling rack or heatproof surface.

Open can carefully and pour into a bowl or glass jar. Whisk to desired consistency and add a pinch of cinnamon or teaspoon of vanilla or almond extracts, if desired. Let cool to room temperature. Refrigerate in an airtight container for up to 1 week.

Warm sauce before making soda.

To make a glass of dulce de leche soda: Scoop 1 scoop of vanilla ice cream into a tall glass, pour ½ cup dulce de leche sauce on top, then top all with seltzer. Serve with sundae spoon.

Sorbet Sodas/ Sparkling Citrus Floats

One can't leave out or ignore refreshing sorbet floats: they are colorful, tangy, sweet, and tasty. There are so many combinations to try, but here are a few of my favorites.

Pineapple Mango Float

Serves 1

2 scoops mango sorbet

⅓ cup pineapple mint syrup (page 69)

6 oz. Seltzer

Scoop sorbet into a tall glass, drizzle pineapple syrup over sorbet, and pour seltzer on top. Stir gently and serve with a sundae spoon.

Raspberry Lemon Float

Serves 1

2 scoops lemon sorbet

⅓ cup raspberry syrup (page 32)

Seltzer

Scoop sorbet into a tall glass, drizzle raspberry syrup over sorbet, and pour seltzer on top. Stir gently and serve with a sundae spoon.

Mint Orange Float

Serves 1

2 scoops orange sorbet

⅓ cup mint syrup (page 40)

Seltzer

Scoop sorbet into a tall glass, drizzle mint syrup over sorbet, and pour seltzer on top. Stir gently and serve with a sundae spoon.

Cocktails

Bold flavors from concentrated syrups make the most of a sophisticated refreshing cocktail. Using different combinations of syrups and spirits, the possibilities are endless. Here are some tantalizing libations to get you started!

Paloma

*This cocktail is pink and fruity and oh so Palm Beach.
These drinks are always on hand and in the bar cart
when my girlfriends pop in. Here's to the good life!*
Serves 4

1 batch pink
grapefruit syrup
(page 28)

1 cup tequila

½ cup Grand
Marnier

Juice of 1 lime

1 cup seltzer

Lime wheels
for garnish

Fill a pitcher halfway with ice. Add
grapefruit syrup, tequila, Grand
Marnier, and lime juice and mix
well. Top with seltzer and pour into
ice-filled glasses. Garnish with lime
wheel and serve.

Pisco Sour

Most recipes call for lemons, but down in Chile, bartenders use key limes. The bite adds a unique spin to the very fine pisco, a grape brandy hailing from South America. A classic cocktail, it is perfect for mixing up a batch for friends anytime. **Serves 4**

8 oz. pisco ABA

4 teaspoons key lime juice

2 oz. simple syrup

2 egg whites

½ cup seltzer

Fill a cocktail shaker halfway with ice. Add pisco, lime juice, simple syrup, and egg whites and shake well. Remove the shaker top, add seltzer, and shake to mix. Strain into coupe glasses and serve.

Razzmatazz

This drink is delightfully crisp with the addition of bitters, which balances the raspberry syrup in all the right places. **Serves 4**

1 batch raspberry
syrup (page 32)

1 cup Campari

2 dashes
orange bitters

1 cup seltzer

Raspberries
for garnish

Fill a cocktail shaker halfway with ice. Add the raspberry syrup, Campari, and bitters, and shake well. Strain into ice-filled rocks glasses and top with seltzer. Garnish with raspberries and serve.

Daiquiri

Rum is a hot trend in mixology right now, and there are many varieties available. Dark rum is stronger in flavor and has more molasses than the lighter counterparts. The daiquiri flavors are inviting and fresh, and adding the bubbles to it makes it effervescent and lively. **Serves 4**

8 oz. dark rum

2 oz. Cointreau

¼ cup freshly squeezed lime juice

3 tablespoons cane sugar

2 cups strawberries, fresh or frozen, washed and hulled

1 cup seltzer

Lime wheels for garnish

Combine rum, Cointreau, lime juice, sugar, and strawberries in a blender and blend until smooth. Add seltzer and blend quickly to mix. Pour into glasses, garnish with lime wheel, and serve.

Mango Daiquiri

Mango nectar is typically a bit sweeter than fresh mangoes. If using fresh, add 3 tablespoons cane sugar to the blender. I've been known to use frozen mangoes here with just as tasty a result. **Serves 4**

8 oz. dark rum

2 oz. Cointreau

2 oz. freshly squeezed lime juice

1 cup mango nectar

1 cup seltzer

Combine rum, Cointreau, lime juice, and mango nectar in a blender and blend until smooth. Add seltzer and blend quickly to mix. Pour into glasses, garnish with a lime wheel, and serve.

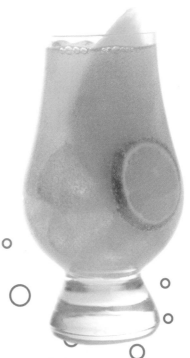

Lemon Lush

This cocktail is tangy and sweet; the limoncello offers a distinctive citrus fragrance. **Serves 4**

1 batch lemon syrup (page 31)

1 cup vodka

½ cup limoncello

1 cup seltzer

Mint sprigs for garnish

Fill a pitcher halfway with ice. Add lemon syrup, vodka, and limoncello, and mix well. Top with seltzer and pour into ice-filled glasses. Garnish with mint sprigs and serve.

Fizzmopolitan

There's something about the combination of gin, orange, and vanilla that makes for a most sunny cocktail, no matter what time of year. **Serves 4**

1 batch blood orange syrup (page 24)

1 cup gin

½ cup Tuaca® liqueur

Juice of 1 lime

1 cup seltzer

Orange peel for garnish

Fill a pitcher halfway with ice. Add blood orange syrup, gin, orange liqueur, and lime juice and mix well. Top with seltzer and pour into martini glasses. Garnish with orange peel and serve.

Whiskey Tango

Whiskey is at the forefront of cocktail couture. It seems everything old is new again. This pairing lends itself nicely to the sweet peach and spicy basil syrup. **Serves 4**

1 batch peach
basil syrup
(page 62)

1 cup whiskey

2 dashes
orange bitters

1 cup seltzer

Basil leaves
for garnish

Fill a pitcher halfway with ice. Add peach basil syrup, whiskey, and bitters and mix well. Top with seltzer and pour into ice-filled rocks glasses. Garnish with basil leaf and serve.

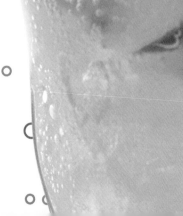

Cuba Libre

Rum and cola are natural companions. This is definitely a craft cocktail with the combo of natural cola syrup. The flavors are more pronounced, fresher, and that leads to a better cocktail. **Serves 4**

1 batch cola syrup (page 17)

1 cup rum

Juice of 1 lime

1 cup seltzer

Lime wedges for garnish

Fill a pitcher halfway with ice. Add the cola syrup, rum, and lime juice and mix well. Top with seltzer. Squeeze a lime wedge into each of 4 ice-filled glasses, pour cocktail, and serve.

Mojito

This is a recipe for purists. Be sure to use fresh lime juice, and go for a superior rum, such as 10 Cane®, Rhum Barbancourt White®, or Mount Gay Reserve®.

1 batch mint syrup (page 40)

Juice of 1 lime

2 limes, cut into wedges

10 mint leaves for muddling, more for garnish

8 oz. rum

¾ cup seltzer

Muddle together mint syrup, lime juice, lime wedges, and mint leaves in a bar glass or pitcher, add rum and ice, and mix. Divide evenly among 4 glasses. Top each drink with seltzer, garnish with mint leaves, and serve.

Appletastic

This is a fall favorite, great for the tailgate, or crisp fall afternoons with friends. **Serves 4**

2 cups apple cider

8 oz. vanilla vodka

4 oz. Tuaca

½ cup seltzer

Fill a pitcher halfway with ice and add the cider, vodka, and Tuaca. Pour evenly into glasses, top with seltzer, and serve.

Classic Bourbon Smash

A classic smash is defined as a fortified wine (but any base spirit can be used) muddled with lemon, mint, and sugar. That's it. Add any spirits, fruit, or syrups to your heart's desire. **Serves 1**

4 lemon wedges

½ oz. agave nectar

6 mint leaves, plus sprig for garnish

2 oz. whiskey or bourbon

Seltzer

Muddle the lemon wedges with the agave nectar and mint leaves in a rocks glass. Add the bourbon and crushed ice. Pour into a cocktail shaker and shake vigorously. Strain back into the rocks glass. Top with seltzer and serve.

Bourbon Grand Smash

Because Grand Marnier is really a cognac infused with orange peels and other spices, it works beautifully in a smash recipe. The orange flavors mellow out the rich bourbon, mixing with the lemon, mint, and nectar, tasting like adult lemonade. **Serves 1**

5 lemon wedges

½ oz. agave nectar

6 mint leaves

2 oz. Grand Marnier

¼ cup seltzer

Muddle the lemon wedges with the agave nectar and mint leaves in a rocks glass. Add the Grand Marnier and crushed ice. Pour into a cocktail shaker and shake vigorously. Strain back into the rocks glass. Top with seltzer and serve.

Blackberry Bramble

The bramble, with its blackberry tang, is celebrated for its fruity kick and refreshing taste. If blackberry doesn't float your boat, swap it out for raspberry, strawberry, orange, or peach liqueur. **Serves 4**

8 blackberries, more for garnish

¼ cup lemon juice

2 oz. agave nectar

8 oz. gin

4 oz. crème de cassis

Seltzer to top

Muddle blackberries with lemon juice and agave nectar in a bar glass. Add gin and crème de cassis, fill with crushed ice, and shake well. Pour into 4 glasses and top each with seltzer. Garnish with blackberries and serve.

Margarita

I always add a splash of pineapple juice to my margs. It seems to mellow and marry all the strong flavors for a spectacular result. I make these sparkling drinks year round. **Serves 4**

Sea salt for salting rims of margarita glasses

½ cup lime syrup (page 30)

1 cup tequila blanco

½ cup Cointreau

¼ cup pineapple juice

½ cup seltzer

Lime wheels for garnish

Salt the rims of 4 margarita glasses. Fill a pitcher halfway with ice, add the lime syrup, tequila, Cointreau, and pineapple juice, and mix well. Divide evenly among 4 ice-filled glasses and top each drink with seltzer. Garnish with a lime wheel and serve.

Gimlet

Light and easy, gimlets are palate friendly and ideal as a year-round cocktail. **Serves 4**

¼ cup mint syrup (page 40)

1 cup vodka

Juice of 2 limes, plus more for garnish

1 cup seltzer

Mint sprig for garnish

Fill a cocktail shaker halfway with ice, add the mint syrup, vodka, and limejuice, and shake well. Strain into 4 glasses. Top each drink with seltzer, garnish with limes and mint sprig, and serve.

Watermelon Crush

This drink is a tangy thirst quencher that I've served at girlfriend gatherings, celebrations, and porch parties.
Serves 4

2 cups watermelon, cubed, plus additional for garnish, if desired

1 cup vodka

4 oz. St. Germain elderflower liqueur

Juice of 1 lime

¼ cup orange juice

1 cup seltzer

Lime wheels for garnish, if desired

Muddle watermelon cubes in a pitcher, add vodka, St. Germain liquor, lime juice, and orange juice and mix well. Add ice and top with seltzer. Pour into glasses, garnish with a lime wheel or watermelon cube, and serve.

Chai Tea/Chai Soda

Chai, derived from a South Asian drink, is a black tea mixed with milk, sugar, and a blend of spices. I find this both soothing and calming, sultry and invigorating. **Serves 2**

4 cups water

Tablespoon sugar

White cardamom pods

4 whole cloves

1 cinnamon stick, cracked

Pinch of nutmeg

2 black tea bags

1½ cups milk

½ cup sweetened condensed milk

½ cup Tuaca or vanilla liqueur

Pinch of nutmeg

1 cup seltzer

Combine the water, sugar, cardamom pods, cloves, cinnamon stick, and nutmeg in a saucepan over medium heat. Bring to a boil and add the tea bags. Lower the heat to a simmer, add the milk and sweetened condensed milk, and simmer for 2 minutes. Remove the pan from the heat and let the mixture cool. Strain the chai tea mixture through a fine-mesh sieve into a bowl and refrigerate until cool.

To make a chai soda: Pour 1 cup chai tea mixture into a glass, add Tuaca liqueur and seltzer, and mix gently. Add ice and serve.

Coffee Conclusion

This is my kind of a coffee cocktail—serious and to the point—blending dessert and a nightcap all in one.
Serves 4

2 cups vanilla gelato

8 oz. Patrón XO Cafe

Seltzer

Sugar cookies for garnish

Scoop ½ cup gelato into each of 4 rocks glasses. Divide the Patrón XO Cafe among the glasses, and then top with seltzer. Garnish with a cookie and serve.

Mixed Berry Mojito

Try this mojito for a sweeter, more up-front flavor mix. The addition of the blackberry liqueur really packs a punch. **Serves 4**

10 mint leaves for muddling, more for garnish

2 limes, cut into wedges

1 batch mixed berry syrup (page 58)

Juice of 1 lime

1 cup rum

½ cup blackberry liqueur

Seltzer

Muddle mint leaves with lime wedges in a bar glass or pitcher, add the berry syrup, lime juice, rum, and blackberry liqueur, and mix well. Divide evenly among 4 glasses and top each drink with seltzer. Garnish with lime wedges and serve.

Passion Fruit Mojito

A zesty combo, the apricot brandy mellows the citrus notes of the passion fruit and lime, leaving nothing but a tropical tingled libation. Better make a batchful.
Serves 4

10 mint leaves for muddling, plus more for garnish

2 limes, cut into wedges

1 batch mint syrup (page 40)

Juice of 2 limes

1 cup rum

½ cup apricot brandy

½ cup passion fruit nectar

Seltzer

Muddle mint leaves, lime wedges, and mint syrup in a bar glass or pitcher, add lime juice, rum, apricot brandy, and passion fruit nectar, and mix well. Divide evenly among 4 glasses and top each drink with seltzer. Garnish with mint leaves and serve.

Pineapple Slush

This party of flavors is a go-to for dock parties, boat rides, or sunset cruises. Just transfer the drinks into an insulated cooler and you're good to go! **Serves 4**

1 cup pineapple mint syrup (page 69) or 2 cups pineapple juice

1 cup light rum

½ cup banana liqueur

½ cup guava nectar

Juice of 2 limes

Seltzer

Pineapple chunks for garnish

Fill a pitcher halfway with ice, add pineapple syrup, rum, banana liqueur, guava nectar, and lime juice, and mix well. Strain into 4 rocks glasses filled with crushed ice. Top with seltzer, garnish with pineapple chunks, and serve.

Frozen Mudslide

A decadent blend of rich liqueurs make this a dreamy concoction, perfect for easing into the weekend. Who needs dessert? **Serves 4**

1 cup Kahlua®

½ cup vanilla vodka

½ cup Baileys Irish Cream®

½ cup whole milk or cream

1 cup seltzer

Whipped cream for topping

Fill a blender with 3 cups ice, add all the ingredients, and blend until smooth. Divide evenly among 4 glasses, top each drink with seltzer and whipped cream (or a Kahlua floater, if preferred), and serve.

Big Bubbly Batches

Because there is nothing that quite says "party" more than a big batch of luscious bubbly concoctions—whether served from a blender, a pitcher, or grandma's punch bowl—you should always have plenty of options on hand. Here is a collection of my favorites.

Pimm's Cup

This traditional English summertime drink with deep, complex flavors is perfect for tennis parties, polo matches, or any backyard hip happening. Pimm's®, an old British standard, is a gin-based spirit made with aromatic herbs that's making its way to the modern cocktail scene. **Serves 8**

3 cups Pimm's

3 cups chilled (page 20) or store-bought ginger ale

3 cups chilled seltzer

Juice of 1 lemon

Juice of 1 lime

¼ cup grenadine

Lemon slices and Maraschino cherries for garnish

Combine all the ingredients (except garnish) in large pitcher or drinks dispenser and mix well. Add ice, garnish with lemon slices and cherries, and serve.

Spanish Sangria

Sangria is traditionally a fruit-based wine libation from Portugal or Spain. Using fresh seasonal fruit adds to the sweetness and fullness of flavor. Use whatever is in season at your local market. **Serves 8**

1 bottle dry red wine, such as merlot or pinot noir

1½ cups Cointreau or orange liqueur

½ cup cognac

¼ cup orange juice

1 apple, sliced

1 orange, sliced

1 cup red grapes, sliced

1 lemon, sliced

1 cinnamon stick

2 cups chilled seltzer

Combine the wine, Cointreau, cognac, fruit, and cinnamon stick in a pitcher and chill for up to 1 hour to allow the flavors to develop. Add the chilled seltzer slowly; then add ice and serve.

Lemon Sangria

The beauty of a sangria recipe is that it is easy, and it's totally up to you as to what you put in the pitcher. Limoncello and elderflower liqueur make this sangria approachable and pleasing with its lemon fragrance and sunny color. **Serves 8**

1 bottle dry white wine

1 cup limoncello liqueur

½ cup St. Germain liqueur

2 tablespoons lime juice

1 kiwi cut into stars

1 lemon sliced into wheels

2 cups seltzer

Pour wine and liqueurs into a pitcher. Slice and add fruit. Let mixture macerate for at least 30 minutes. Slowly top with seltzer, add ice, and serve.

Sangria Tropical

Island dreaming lead to the addition of passion fruit liqueur in this tropical punch. The pear liqueur balances out the sweetness and marries perfectly with the fruit for a winning result. **Serves 8**

1 bottle dry white wine

½ cup passion fruit liqueur

½ cup pear liqueur

1 cup pineapple chunks

Juice of 1 lime

1 orange, sliced

1 kiwi, sliced

½ cup mango chunks

Chilled seltzer

Combine all the ingredients, except the seltzer, in a pitcher and chill for up to 1 hour to allow the flavors to develop. Add the chilled seltzer slowly; then add ice, and serve.

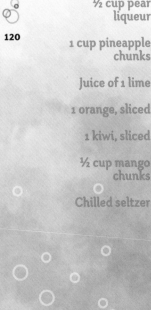

Bloody Mary

The old standby for breakfast, brunch, or afternoon gatherings never seems to get old, especially with the addition of lime juice for extra citrus zip. The seltzer is effervescently divine. **Serves 4**

2 cups tomato juice

1 cup vodka

3 tablespoons Worcestershire sauce

Juice of 1 lime

2 tablespoons prepared horseradish

1 teaspoon hot pepper sauce

1 teaspoon salt

1 teaspoon freshly ground pepper

Seltzer

Celery, olives, cherry tomatoes to garnish

Fill a cocktail shaker with ice and add the tomato juice, vodka, Worcestershire sauce, lime juice, horseradish, hot pepper sauce, and salt and pepper. Shake well, remove the top, and add the seltzer. Shake again, and strain into ice-filled glasses. Garnish with celery, olives, and cherry tomatoes and serve.

Pink Petal Punch/
Pink Lady Punch

This is a festive punch for casual gatherings, showers, and luncheons. It's super easy to mix up, looks pretty, and puts everyone is a flirty mood. **Serves 8**

2 cups guava nectar

½ cup apricot brandy

2 cups vodka

4 cups lemon lime soda (page 23)

Fresh raspberries and lemon slices for ice ring garnish

Combine guava nectar, brandy, and vodka in a drinks dispenser or punch bowl. Slowly top with lemon-lime soda. Garnish with ice ring.

To make ice ring: Use a plastic container or a bundt pan. Arrange fruit on bottom of container or pan. Fill halfway with water. Place in freezer for up to 4 hours to let set. Place second half of fruit on top of ice, fill with water, and freeze.

Planter's Punch

History has it that Caribbean plantation owners sipped this libation on their porches after a day overseeing the land. A mix of rums, citrus, and sugar, this punch is by nature open to interpretation. Here is a true crowd-pleasing combination. **Serves 8**

4 cups dark rum (use several different varieties to spice things up)

1 batch pineapple mint syrup (page 69)

½ cup lime juice

4 cups freshly squeezed orange juice

¼ cup grenadine

3 cups seltzer

Pineapple wedges and orange wheels for garnish

Fill a large pitcher or punch bowl with ice and add rum, pineapple syrup, lime juice, orange juice, and grenadine. Top with seltzer, garnish with pineapple wedges and orange wheels, and serve.

Rum Runner

*A taste of the tropics with bright flavors, this is a
winning combination of tropical fruit juices and rum.*
Serves 4

1 cup Bacardi
dark rum

½ cup blackberry
brandy

½ cup banana
liqueur

2 cups pome-
granate juice

¼ cup grenadine

¼ cup lime juice

2 cups seltzer

Fill a blender halfway with ice and
add all the ingredients, except
seltzer. Blend until smooth. Pour into
a glass, add seltzer, and serve.

Index

About the Author

Colleen Mullaney is the author of 11 lifestyle and cocktail books, including *Preschool Parties: Easy Ideas for Princesses, Pirates & Other Little People*; *It's Five O' Clock Somewhere: The Global Guide to Fabulous Cocktails*; *Punch*; *Fairy Parties*; and *The Stylish Girl's Guide to Fabulous Cocktails*. Colleen began her career as the Editor-in-Chief of *Family Circle Homecrafts*, *FTD in Bloom*, *Jo-Ann Etc*, and *At Home with Chris Madden* magazines. Her crafting books cover the range of her crafting expertise in floral design, home decorating, entertaining, and various crafts and include *Crafting On the Go: Shells*; *Crafting On the Go: Felt; Faux Fabulous Florals*; and *One-of-a-Kind Weddings*. Colleen lives in Westchester, New York.